FLATTENING THE HAMSTER WHEEL

Stop Grinding and Start Making an Impact

CONTENTS

CHAPTER 1 3
CHAPTER 2 10
CHAPTER 3 14
CHAPTER 4 24
CHAPTER 5 32
CHAPTER 6 44
CHAPTER 7 56
CHAPTER 8 66
CHAPTER 9 79
CHAPTER 10 97
CHAPTER 11 104
CHAPTER 12 113
CHAPTER 13 122
MORE HELP TO DO GREAT THINGS 128

Flattening the Hamster Wheel
Copyright © 2019 by Matthew Rouse

All rights reserved. No part of this book may be reproduced in any form or by any electronic or mechanical means including information storage and retrieval systems, without permission in writing from the author. The only exception is by a reviewer, who may quote short excerpts in a review.

Cover designed by Matthew Rouse
Editing by Kari Rouse
Last edit Michelle De Lude
Back Cover Photo by Craig Brubaker
v1.0

Matthew Rouse
Visit my website at hookseo.com

Printed in the United States of America

First Printing: September 2019

ISBN- 9781088890226

For Faith, who deserved more of my time, so I figured out how to make that happen.

CHAPTER 1
Janet Needs a Vacation

*"When you don't know what matters most,
anything makes sense."*
—Gary Kellar

I WANT TO INTRODUCE YOU TO JANET, who happens to be one of my best customers.

When I am doing workshops or speaking at events, I often talk about Janet. It turns out, everyone knows someone like Janet. Maybe you will know a Janet too.

Janet is in her late thirties and has two children who are 8 and 10 years old. They do a lot of family things together but one thing their entire family enjoys is Tae Kwon Do classes. Janet isn't just someone's mom; Janet could kick your ass if she had to.

If you're friends with Janet on one of her social media platforms you will see a lot of photos of her kids, only surpassed by shared posts about coffee, funny parenting related memes, wine and the odd inspirational quote.

Because she is a small business owner, she also shares a lot of memes that say things like...

When you buy from a Mom & Pop Business, you are not helping a CEO buy a third vacation home.

You are helping a little girl get dance lessons, a little boy get his team jersey, a mom or dad put food on the table, pay a mortgage, or a student pay for college.

Or something like this...

I can't wait for the day that I can drink wine with the kids instead of because of them.

Janet is the "Office Manager" (and owner) of a small plumbing business in town. Her husband is a plumber by trade, and they have three other employees. They are doing well but it takes a lot of hustle and a lot of hours to keep everyone working and make payroll, etc.

Janet is time poor.

She is handling the business, the phone calls, booking jobs, bookkeeping, HR, managing her website, trying to market the business, and she even cleans the office. If something needs to be done that isn't plumbing, Janet does it.

Janet is tired.

Not just physically tired from running the business and her household and taking care of the kids. Janet needs a vacation but who has the time?

She wants to stop doing things that are a waste of time, but she's scared that if she doesn't do *everything* that her business will fail. She will let down her employees, her husband, and her family.

Janet is stressed.

She tries to be healthy, but because of the time crunch she's always under, she doesn't eat right, she's gaining some weight, she isn't sleeping enough or sleeping well. It's all just taking its toll on her.

She's getting fed up with it all. She's usually a positive, happy person, but she's getting irritable, and the seams are starting to show a little.

Sound familiar?

Janet is on the Hamster Wheel when it comes to her business and her marketing. She is checking off tasks day after day, but she never seems to get ahead.

But there is something else you should know about Janet…

She isn't a real person.

Janet is my customer avatar.

When I think about writing books like this one, or marketing services my company offers to small businesses, I "speak" to Janet.

I know where Janet hangs out online. I know what her goals and hopes and challenges and values are.

Understanding Janet is the key to being able to focus my efforts and not end up on the Hamster Wheel along with people like Janet. Let's face it, most business owners and managers are like Janet.

A customer avatar is a persona you make up for a potential customer for your business. It's an imaginary friend for your sales and marketing. Knowing your customer is half the battle.

The illusion of productivity is the other half.

Imagine a hamster wheel that is wired up to power a lightbulb. When the hamster runs, the light will shine, but when the hamster stops running, the light goes off.

This is how most business tasks are accomplished. They provide limited, short term gains that need constant attention, like stoking a fire. If you stop adding wood, the flames go out and your business will get cold.

Most of us have what Roland Frasier refers to as, "*The Dancing Bear problem.*"

We're all basically just Dancing Bears.

When we're *doing the dance*, we bring in sales. But if we stop dancing, the money stops coming in.

We can't leave because there is no one else to run on the hamster wheel that is driving the business. We can't take vacations and most days we can't even leave on time.

We can never get all our tasks done, leaving us feeling like we're working ourselves to death but never accomplishing anything.

We can't sell our business because we're not building repeat clients or a machine that runs without us, so we can never retire.

If this sounds like you, you're not alone. This is how most businesses big and small operate and it's not sustainable over a long period of time.

It's time to *Flatten the Hamster Wheel* and become more productive and more effective in our businesses so that we can be more than just *Dancing Bears*.

Do it for yourself.

Do it for Janet.

Because you and Janet both need a vacation.

CHAPTER 2
How did we get here?

"Our job is not to create content. Our job is to change the world of the people who consume it."
—Andrea Fryrear

WHEN I WAS ABOUT 12 YEARS OLD, Dungeons & Dragons was starting to get popular with nerdy kids and I was in the thick of it.

I lived in a small mining town called Elkford in a valley in south eastern British Columbia, Canada.

We had one stop light. We had one convenience store. And if you wanted to rent a VHS movie, you had to drive for an hour to another town that had a 7-11 with movie rentals.

To say the least, there wasn't a lot to do once you got your hiking and camping fix. And trust me, when you literally live on the side of a mountain in a forest, camping isn't your number one vacation choice anymore.

The thing about Dungeons & Dragons was that it was a new kind of game. No one had invented a game like this ever before. There is no winner or loser. It's a group of friends working together to create an interactive fiction.

It is the process of inventing a story as a group.

The Dungeon Master is basically a combination of referee and storyteller. She creates a world for the players to interact in and interprets the actions of the players based on the rules. The main characters in the story are the other players and you never know what they will do next.

The better the "atmosphere" of the world, the more engaged the players and the better the story becomes.

It's all about the story.

As a young teen in a small town, this gripped me completely and my friends and I spent most of our free time playing games, creating worlds, and building stories. Some stories we would remember our entire lives.

What made your *game worlds* rich and compelling were the characters. Just like any good story, you need to have good characters. These were called NPCs, or *non-player characters*.

I would spend hours meticulously writing their backgrounds.

- What did they look and sound like?
- What did they know or not know?
- What were their abilities and occupations?
- What were their motivations?

These are the things that go into creating what we call in the marketing world, a *customer avatar*. A way to make up a fictional version of a customer, dare I say, a *non-player customer* or *NPC*.

We're going to walk through a simple exercise on how to make a customer avatar but first I want you to know why it's so important… even if you've done it before.

Because I am trying to save you time, we are going to just do the important bits, and you can fill in more of the details later.

How is this going to save you time and make your company grow?

Stay with me. It'll all come together soon.

CHAPTER 3
Know Your Customer

"You are asking a prospect to make an investment of the most valuable things they have, time and money."
—Russ Henneberry

WHAT MAKES YOUR CUSTOMER AVATAR REAL ARE THE PARTS THAT PEOPLE SKIP WHEN THEY MAKE CUSTOMER AVATARS. They write down an age range and income and rub their hands together, thinking they've got the job done.

"Their Janet" is a 35 to 55-year-old woman whose family earns 100k-500k a year and likes good customer service and shopping. Yeah, that "perfect" customer is also every other brand on the planet's perfect customer too.

It's like saying that your skin care product is perfect for "anyone with skin," or you're a mechanic for "anyone who drives a vehicle."

But it isn't, is it?

Take the mechanic example.

- Do you work on *every* kind of car?
- What about golf carts? Freightliners?
- What about people with no money?
- What about people who have a Bentley, McLaren, or Lamborghini? Are you insured to work on those?
- What about people who live in a different city?

I could go on...

Can we agree that "everyone" is not your customer? And they *really* aren't your perfect customer.

The idea here is not to try to cast a wide net, but to focus on the people who are the best fit for your business. It doesn't mean we *can't* help those who don't fit the perfect-customer-mold; it just means we aren't focusing our efforts on finding them.

Now back to building our Customer Avatar.

It's important to know that my Avatar, Janet, has two tween aged children and takes Tae Kwon Do. It gives her depth as a character. It makes her more real, and therefore, it's easier to talk to her as a real person.

The goal here is to have a character that is real enough that we can imagine ourselves talking to them.

When I post something on social media, write an email newsletter, or even when I look for guests or topics for our videos or podcast, I ask myself, "What would Janet want to know?"

Take a moment and think about what your perfect customer would look like.

- Are they male or female or non-binary?
- What do they do for a living?
- What do they wear?

- Where do they shop?
- How do they talk? Do they use slang/profanity?
- Married? Kids? Pets?

You're building a picture of this person in your mind. Now give *your Janet* a name.

If there were a cocktail party and you met *your Janet*, what would you say to one another? How would the conversation start?

What's on their mind? What movies, or shows do they like? What books have they read? What are their hobbies?

And just like a real cocktail party, they may bring up a problem they have that your business can solve.

How do you explain your business to them?

You don't say, "I have a sale on tires! Buy my tires! 20$ off this week only!"

But that's what most businesses are doing on social media and in their mailing lists. It immediately puts people's guard up, and it erodes their trust in you and your brand.

It's lazy marketing and it's working less and less every day. The average person can see through a self-serving sales pitch a mile away and literally sees thousands of them every day.

So how do you stand out?

Let's pretend you do own a tire store. What would you say?

I heard you say your car was slipping around on the road in the rain and you almost crashed. That's got to be super scary.

I used to hate to drive in the rain.

One time I was driving down the freeway and it was late and dark, and the kid was asleep in the back seat and then I saw this truck coming around the corner and it just started sliding sideways over the center lane.

It was like time suddenly slowed down! That ever happen to you?

I swerved and got out of the way just in time. It was a very close call. I almost had to pull over and check my shorts!

Anyway, I had these new rain tires on my car that stop your car from sliding as much on wet pavement. You should come check them out at the shop. Here's my card if you want to drop by sometime and I'll give you the grand tour.

But that was sure scary. I hugged my kid so tightly when I got home!

Your product story could just as easily be in an email, or in a social media post, with a photo of a dark, rainy roadway at night.

I guarantee you'll sell more tires with that story then trying to get people to join your email or social media account to be bombarded every week with *Tire Sale! Tire Sale! Tire Sale!*

When I email my list for Hook SEO Digital Marketing, I always start with a story. It could be a few sentences, or even a few pages. But I always start with a story.

Once I talked about how I was shocked to find out when my ex-girlfriend in high school was dating one of my best friends because I walked into his house one night and her shoes were at the door. (I grew up in a part of Canada where people don't lock their doors.)

One story was a short "investigative" piece about what background music or ambient noise is most effective for doing creative work. (If you're curious, it's low ambient noise with soft music, but we'll get into that more in the chapter on personal productivity.)

This didn't take a vast amount of research. A few Google searches and skimming a couple articles and I am ready to drop some helpful knowledge to my readers.

What I almost never talk about is how Search Engine Optimization really works. Why? Because it's boring for most people.

I might explain some of the very high-level concepts, but I don't get into the nitty gritty about building page authority and how 301 redirects work. I can already see your eyes glazing over.

I know those things and to a professional person in my industry, those things are just the basics. But they are too much in the weeds for my clients, and honestly, they aren't interesting or entertaining to most people. Companies hire me to *know* those things. Not to *tell them* about those things.

Remember, you want to write what your readers want to read, not what you want to tell them.

Then you get the chance to do a little education at the same time, and maybe mention something important that is going on.

For example, I am writing an in-depth course to teach email marketing. I will mention it sometimes to my audience, but my emails are never, "BUY MY COURSE!"

There is always a story, insight, or something they want or need that I can provide. Because you're not just "creating value," as you will see plastered all over the Internet by all the "gurus."

You are building a relationship with your audience. You're that friend who's an expert in your field. You are the friend people want to take out for coffee to pick your brain.

And if you want to do that "at scale," you must use email or another form of one-to-many communication.

Something magical happens when I keep that in mind.

People reply to my marketing emails.

They comment on my posts.

They start conversations with me and others.

They talk about the things I write with other people. We are all building relationships.

As Seth Godin would say, "they tell *the others*." *The others* are the people who *get it*. The ones who are also my perfect customer.

That's hard to do when all you're putting in your emails is "Tires 20% Off This Week Only!"

Talking to people directly and knowing a lot about the people your business deals with isn't very scalable, but that's not a bad thing.

David Gadlin talked about this when I interviewed him on Episode 30 of the Digital Marketing Masters Podcast.

"When you're growing a business, and starting a business, do things that aren't scalable. Because you build that loyalty with those people you do it with that will help you scale down the road."

You want to be someone's smart friend, like someone they ask to take to coffee to "pick their brain." Not just another piece of junk mail in a world buried in junk mail and spam already.

CHAPTER 4
Opportunity Costs

"Opportunity cost is the key to making decisions. Once you know the value of the alternatives you're giving up, you can be smarter about what you're choosing to do."
—Seth Godin

I STILL CALL MY DAUGHTER BABY FAITH, even though at the time of printing this book, she's a 3.5-year-old human and well into her Toddler status.

Yesterday, Baby Faith was watching the show *Boss Baby: Back in Business* on Netflix, based on the original Boss Baby movie.

The objective of the "corporation" in Boss Baby is *to* "increase baby love." The babies have a secret mission to make people love babies more than cats, puppies, or the elderly.

I'm proud to say it's her favorite show. Cartoons and business together? What more could a toddler ask for?

In one episode, the main character, *Boss Baby*, is trying to get his brother to focus on the bigger picture and says, "You're chasing nickels around a $20 Bill!"

Some business books say things like, "Stepping over a dollar to pick up a dime."

The idea is simple.

You should not be doing low-profit work at the expense of high-profit work. But how do you make sure you're doing high-profit work?

The magic here is in the Opportunity Cost.

There are several types of opportunity cost.

The easiest way to define it is this.

"The loss of a potential gain from other alternatives when one alternative is chosen."

Let's go over some examples.

If you invest in a savings account that is 0.1% interest when you could put that money into an investment account that makes 3% interest. The Opportunity Cost is that 2.9% you didn't earn by taking the safer investment.

You could get up and beat the traffic, but you hit the snooze button three times, and then spent an extra 30 minutes in traffic. Those 3 snoozes cost you 30 minutes in rush hour.

In your businesses, working for an hour to think up your Social Media posts, getting the right photos and text, and posting them. Then changing your mind about what to say four times and editing your posts and then hitting refresh every 5 minutes to see if anyone has "liked" it yet, isn't very productive work. Especially when only a dozen people will see it, if you're lucky.

The Opportunity Cost is the 100 customers you could have reached writing an email instead. Or you could have determined one customer you already have that could use more of what your company offers and saying, "Hello."

One more example, this time about doing the math before we leap into things. I'll keep the dollar amounts low to keep the math easy.

Setting up an event for 20 people at $20 a person sounds like you're going to make $400.

But if the food, drinks, advertising and room rent cost you $350, then what you're actually making is $50.

If making money is your goal, you could have consulted with 1 person for a couple of hours at $50/hr and doubled your money with way less work.

Now if building relationships with 20 potential customers is your goal, then congratulations, you just met 20 new people for $50.

The best way to sort out opportunity cost is to analyze what you're doing before you do it. And to ask yourself, "What is this action for?"

And you should also ask, "How much will this cost me? And is the cost worth the time and risk involved?"

"If I am going to commit to doing this, what else could I be doing that has more value?"

"What is the long-term value of this task?"

Or as *Boss Baby* would say, "How does this increase baby love?" Your tasks should be in-line with your long-term goals and you should understand the Opportunity Cost of each business action.

* * *

"People who understand compound interest earn it. Those who don't, pay it." - Eric Siu

Is the task you are doing a one-time benefit, or will it produce long term benefits that compound over time?

Meeting people *one to one* takes a lot of time and energy, but relationships pay off over the long term. If you keep meeting more people, networking, making connections, those kinds of connections will pay off the more you have.

A network's value increases as more people are connected to it. Growing your network is a long-term win.

Writing in-depth emails or blog articles are a great way to connect with people, but I also turn mine into future social media posts, blogs, Medium articles, and podcasts. Some of them even end up being expanded into chapters in books (wink).

The original effort is compounded by the ability to repurpose the research and content later.

Any time you can compound your efforts, just like compound interest, that's a task worth doing.

* * *

There are other problems with Opportunity Costs that are hidden from view. You need to flip the script on these problems and turn them into opportunities.

When you are busy working on the daily grind of your business, you aren't making anything new. New products, new connections, new opportunities.

Also, telling yourself you're just going to sleep less or work even more hours isn't a good long-term solution. By delegating tasks, or removing low-value tasks from your workload, you are giving yourself the ability to work on new things.

Can you better leverage employees or virtual assistants to help you get more done? Maybe there is work they can do just as well as you can, or better, to free up your time to work on tasks of a greater value to your growing business.

Saying Yes to doing a presentation or event could help you network with more people at once. Partnerships can help you reach new audiences and build even more relationships. For more on this, read my book, *Start Saying Yes*.

Before you write up another mile-long task list you won't finish, instead ask yourself, *"What can I do right now that will move the business forward?"*

That is what you should be doing.

And equally important, if not more important is, *"What should I stop doing?"*

Coming up, we will talk more about ways to determine which things you should be doing.

Remember that mastering how to determine Opportunity Costs allows you to do the most beneficial tasks and get the most benefit and productivity out of the time you have.

CHAPTER 5
Don't Let Sunk Costs Sink You

"Humans are highly risk averse creatures, so we tend to prefer NOT losing something over potentially gaining something, even if we don't like what we would lose."
—Dr. Liz Powell

MOST PEOPLE DON'T WANT TO CHANGE PHONE CARRIERS. That's why the deals to switch are so good. It's hard to get someone to switch, but once they do, they are going to stay with their new carrier for a long time.

You probably need to get a new phone, but you just spent all that time getting your apps organized and your settings just right. You might not be able to port your number over to a new carrier, and all your friends have your current phone number.

And is your carrier that bad? Just because you pay twice as much now as you would pay somewhere else?

You will have to call your provider and the new carrier to switch. Plus, you probably need to drive to the cell phone shop and wait there while they move over all your personal information to the new phone. It's just a pain.

There are two forces at work here stopping you from making the financially sound decision to get a new phone carrier with a cheaper plan, better service, etc.

Sunk Costs – Cost in time, money, or emotional effort that you have already invested and cannot recover.

Switching Cost - Cost in time, money, or emotional effort it will take to change to a new provider or system.

There is also a third factor at work, and this is why companies are falling over themselves to get you to switch from your existing carrier to them.

They are selling to you at an initial loss because they know the *Average Lifetime Value* of a customer. They know that people don't want to change once they get a new phone carrier because of the pain of switching and the sunk cost effect. Once you move, you are unlikely to move carriers again any time soon.

If they need you to be a customer for six months to start making a profit, who cares? They know the average customer stays for 28 months.

They can spend six months' worth of profit to get you to switch, because the chances are, you will stay with them for much longer and they will make back all the profit on the following 22 months you are paying them.

By taking a loss up front, they can pay more to acquire a customer. Then it's up to their customer success team and their customer retention strategies to keep you on board and make money.

As marketing speaker and author, Dan Kennedy says, *"The business that can spend the most to acquire a customer wins."*

This is because a business that uses the power of betting against the customer lifetime value instead of the profit on the first sale, will win every time.

They will win because they can spend more on marketing. They will spend more up-front time with potential clients because they understand the long-term benefits. They will build relationships because they don't have to make all their money back on the first sale.

Someone is reading this right now and telling themselves, "But in my business, we only do one transaction." such as a real estate deal, or a car, or a piece of manufacturing equipment or a bathroom remodel.

This idea has been tested and works in nearly every industry and in every vertical. The more time, the more money, *the greater the investment* into a potential customer, the more likely you will acquire them.

The greater the investment, the more likely they will stay your customer longer, and the more likely that customer will be to refer you to their friends and family.

* * *

We've all heard the phrase, "*It's lonely at the top.*"

Most people interpret this as a person who's famous or successful, and they are emotionally disconnected from the rest of society. Maybe because people are always trying to use their fame and wealth for their own purposes, or to trick them into something.

Well it may be lonely at the top. But in marketing, it's lonely at the top and that's a good thing. That's where you *want* to be.

Because when it comes to getting the best clients, and not fighting with everyone else at the bottom for table scraps, it's lonely at the top because there isn't as much competition there.

Everyone is fighting to get every potential customer's attention.

They are using every "free" tactic under the sun that they can find in a post or blog. They are all fighting with each other to get clients at little to no cost. And the truth is, most of those people aren't the clients you want anyway.

Now ask yourself one question.

What's the cost of free?

How much does it cost you to keep banging away at social media and free networking groups and posting your cards on bulletin boards or throwing something out on every new app or program that comes along?

What is the cost of your time?

What is the cost of the things you aren't doing, because you're spending time to save money?

The magic trick is, you aren't saving money at all.

You're losing money.

When you are first starting out and you have basically no budget, maybe you have more time than money. But once your business starts to grow, you get stuck. Often, you're stuck because you're using start-up tactics in a maturing business.

What got you here, isn't always what will get you to the next stage.

I've heard that the "One and Threes" are the hardest. This is an often-touted term in startup blogs and books.

They are talking about yearly revenue goals. Getting to 100k, then 300k, then 1M, then 3M, etc. What got you to 300k are not the same tactics that will get your revenue to break a million dollars.

Let's use an example on a popular social media site. The average business post gets shown to 0.17% of your followers. That is 17 people for every 1000 followers you have. However, if you spent just $1 a day advertising that same post, you would reach all 1000 followers in less than a week.

Same amount of time spent creating the post, you just put some gas in it by spending a few dollars.

Better yet, give the direction and budget to your administrator or advertising agency and let them get the job done for you.

Meanwhile, you can focus on making sales or improving your processes, talking to important repeat clients, following up with previous clients… things that make you more money. In this scenario, you are getting able to do more in the same amount of time.

You can't replicate yourself, so you have to hire and delegate.

I interviewed business and executive coach Kerry Walls and she said, "People think by doing these tasks they are saving money, but they're not. They're losing money."

You are losing money because of the *opportunity cost*.

By saving a few dollars to handle social media, you're losing a small fortune in lost productivity elsewhere.

* * *

Don't let sunk costs sink you.

This guy I know has been divorced 5 times.

He was divorced 5 times by the time he was 35 years old. Everyone asked him why he got married 5 times or why he'd been divorced 5 times. It was extraordinary.

"I fall in love too easily," he would tell people. "Things just didn't work out."

But I didn't have the same question as everyone else, I asked, "How did you convince the third, fourth, and fifth women to marry you when you had just been divorced?"

"Every time I knew it wasn't going to work, I got divorced. No use dragging it out. I used it as a chance to start over."

Sure, maybe he was a terrible husband, or bad at choosing the right potential mate for himself, but that's not what's important in this context.

The important part is that when he *knew* his marriage was doomed to failure, he didn't drag it out any longer. He cut his losses and started over.

Last I heard, he was happily married again. Sometimes in love and business, the 6th time's a charm.

Most people will try to make things work in failing relationship or business, and I am not telling you that you shouldn't try.

When it comes to your business's *processes* and *marketing tactics*, you should stop when you know they aren't going to work.

It doesn't matter how long you've been doing it or how much you've invested in it. If it's not working, doing it more will just make you lose time and money faster.

"We're still running radio ads, but I don't think we've gotten a single sale from them in the last year."

I had a customer tell me that recently.

"So why are you still doing it?" I asked them.

"We've been doing it for 10 years and it used to work."

It used to work.

It used to work but there is no proof it works anymore. What you want to do is turn it off and see if business dies down. If it doesn't, don't do it anymore.

If there is no question in your mind that something is no longer working (or never worked), you have three choices:

1. Stop doing it.

2. Change the strategy.

3. Keep wasting your time and money.

I also want to touch briefly on why businesses fail. There are a lot of reasons. I've seen businesses die for reasons ranging from divorce, to poor financial management, to not planning for taxes, litigation, and even some that failed because one or more of the owners had serious drug problems.

What we're talking about here are business processes, productivity and marketing. I am assuming you have most of the other aspects covered already, such as accounting, tax advice, insurance, etc.

These aspects are just as important. Please make sure you seek out professional advice on these topics if you have a need for help in those areas.

* * *

There's a lot to unpack in this chapter. Let's summarize.

How you change your business forever is to stop doing what's not working.

Change what you're doing to something else more effective, even if there is a cost of switching because the pain and cost of switching is almost always less than the opportunity cost.

It will usually cost you less to try something new than to stick with something that you suspect is not working.

The real problem is how do you decide what's not working and figure out what to try next.

And that's why there's still more book to read.

CHAPTER 6
ICCE & ARMAR

"You can't Google relationships."
—Roland Frasier

THE ACRONYMS ICCE AND ARMAR WILL CHANGE YOUR BUSINESS FOREVER, IF YOU FOLLOW THEM. These two simple acronyms are how you make decisions on what you should do next to grow your business. They are so simple, you won't understand why no one told you them before.

I.C.C.E.

This stands for Impact, Confidence, Cost, and Effort. For each idea you come up with to grow your business, you need to do an ICCE Analysis. You should be listing all the ideas in a spreadsheet or on paper.

I like doing them on paper to start with because it helps with retention.

Draw 6 Columns.

One for your idea, and then 4 columns to enter the Impact, Confidence, Cost, and Effort scores. The final column will be for the total score of that idea.

Impact – How much impact will this idea have on your business goals?

Confidence – How confident are you that the idea will work?

Cost – How much money or resources is it going to cost to make this idea happen?

Effort – How much time do you have to commit to making this idea work?

Each of these would be a column in a list or spreadsheet. You will use these to determine what is the best course of action shortly.

But first you need to determine what marketing goals you should tackle first using "ARMAR."

ARMAR

ARMAR is a way to classify ideas that you will use to perform an ICCE Analysis on.

In non-business speak, that means you will be choosing a goal for your business and then determining what actions you need to take to achieve that goal.

A.R.M.A.R. stands for Acquisition, Revenue, Monetization, Activation, and Retention.

I don't want to get into too much theory, but you will need to know what each of these terms is referring to, so you can pick the right one for your business to focus on next.

Acquisition – Get more leads or prospects. This isn't to be confused with sales. This is leads.

Retention – Keep your existing customers longer.

Monetization - Sell more things to the customers you already have.

Activation – Sell things to your new leads. A good example of this would be converting YouTube subscribers into paying customers. Or converting people who come to an event into paying customers.

Revenue – Find new sources of revenue. Most likely creating a new product or service to sell to your new or existing customers.

Now that we know what they are, let's talk about when to use them. We will go over some examples, and chat about which most businesses need to work on.

You will want to list out all the tools and tactics you want to try for a specific topic and then do an **ICCE analysis** on each of these. That will let you know what to try first.

These are listed in the order you should analyze them in your business to try to get unstuck.

Acquisition

If your phone is not ringing, you need *acquisition*. You need more leads. You can't sell if you don't have leads.

This is mistakenly where most people spend all their time. If you're still in business, you're probably already pretty good at customer acquisition and you could grow faster spending more time on something else.

Acquisition strategies are things like events, networking, advertising, cold calling, etc.

Retention

If you have lots of customers coming in the door, but also many customers leaving, you need to work on *retention*.

This is also called *churn rate.* How many of your total customers are leaving compared to how many customers you have total. Lowering *churn* is a valuable strategy to increase profits because it's more expensive to acquire a new customer than it is to keep one.

How can you keep your customers as customers for longer?

A good example of this would be a loyalty program. Another would be trying to communicate more regularly with your existing customers and sell them the value you provide to them already. Meet and greet events, continuity groups, email newsletters, personal attention, and holiday cards, all fall into retention strategies.

Monetization

Most businesses sell more than one product or service. The idea of monetization is to sell more of your products to the customers you already have.

This seems like it should be common knowledge, but you would be surprised how little it is used in practice.

Look at the products and services you have and figure out which of your existing customers would be a fit. Then reach out to them and see if they have the need.

Sometimes it can be as simple as an email.

"Hey Janet. I was thinking about your business and I know you send a monthly email newsletter to your clients. Did you know that our company can write and send those emails on your behalf?"

Activation

You spent all the time trying to get subscribers, followers, fans, etc. But why aren't they all your customers?

It's because you need two steps, *acquisition* and then *activation*.

Acquisitions are about getting someone's attention and getting them to a place where they will hear from you again on a regular basis, such as becoming an email subscriber or a social media follower.

Activation is turning those people into customers and this take different strategies.

Activations can be as simple as letting your fans know that you have a new product or that you have improved a product or service you already provide for your customers.

It could be an event where you invite your prospects to test your product or see how it's manufactured, or demonstrate the equipment used to provide a service.

It could even be a drop campaign by email where you sell the value and ask people to sign up at the end. Maybe it's a charity event you are donating to or partnering at and they can purchase your product through a charity auction.

The tactics are limited only by your imagination and budget. But you should be thinking about getting paying customers in two steps.

Using an advertisement to get someone to sign up for a free product trial is an acquisition strategy. Teaching them to use your product to solve their problem and encouraging them to sign up after the free trial is an activation.

I know it's confusing but trust me. Thinking of these as two steps will help you adjust your strategies.

Revenue

Everyone wants revenue, but in this case, we're talking about creating new streams of revenue. Let's do some examples.

If you sell a product, could you add a warranty?

If you sell a service to help dentists invest in real estate, could you create another service to help them connect with a property management company?

If you sell skin cream, could you also sell sunscreen?

If you sell coaching to business leaders, could you also sell employee group coaching for their staff?

Just ask yourself this question.

"What else can I provide that my existing customers also need?"

Or better yet, ask them!

You can use a couple questions in an email, ask in person or on the phone, or use an email survey tool to discover what other problems your customers are experiencing.

If you have salespeople or support people, ask them for common questions they hear which you could develop into a new product or service that could help them with that issue.

For example, my original web design company years ago, added SEO services when customers kept asking how they can get their new websites to rank higher in search engines.

* * *

The magic trick here is that it isn't magic at all.

With these two simple tools, ARMAR and ICCE, you can identify what your company needs to focus on and what tactic to try first.

Write down each idea on your six-column sheet we created earlier.

Write the idea in column 1.

Column 2-4: Give the idea a score of 1 to 10.

- How much **Impact** do you think the idea will have on your business?
- How much **Confidence** do you have that the idea will work?
- How much will it **Cost** to implement your idea?
- How much **Effort** will be required to make the idea a reality?

The last column is for a total.

Add the **Impact** and **Confidence** together.

Add the **Cost** and **Effort** scores together.

Subtract the *Total Cost and Effort* from the *Total Impact and Confidence*. This is the final **Idea Score**.

Now pick the idea with the highest number, and that's what you should do first.

If that doesn't work, you just move to the next highest ranked tactic on the list.

If you have partners or staff, you can even have different people or departments working on different strategies.

Marketing and sales teams can work on acquisitions and activations, while finance and leadership teams can work on monetization and revenue strategies. Customer service or customer success teams can work on retention.

With these tools at your disposal, you should be able to both identify what you have been doing that is working, what isn't working, and what to try next.

CHAPTER 7
Positioning is Everything and so is Process

"Talent is great but being in the right place at the right time is better."
—Endale Edith

IN A GOLD RUSH, THE PERSON WHO MAKES THE MOST MONEY IS THE ONE WHO SELLS THE SHOVELS. Usually someone finds some gold, and then buys the rights to prospect for it.

By selling the gold and often spending the money frivolously, the rumor mill soon follows.

And the "gold rush" is on.

The first couple prospectors get the easily retrievable gold. From there, the rest have to dig a lot, spend long hours and lots of money to find their fortune in an ever-shrinking amount of gold to find.

They dig until it becomes cost prohibitive and they must shut down. Then someone else comes along to mine that gold.

The winner is the one who "sells the shovels" or mining equipment as a more modern example. The ones who own the hotels and the taverns and the shops that support the gold rush industries.

If you are a gold prospector, you are constantly fighting to find the gold. You must keep digging until you strike it rich or until you can dig no longer. But you must keep "buying more shovels" if you want to keep digging.

The reason selling shovels works is because it's a business process. You can sell them at a premium because you're in the wilderness and there's no Amazon to bring you a shovel with free Prime shipping.

The two things at work here are *positioning* and *process*.

You need something that is consistent, repeatable, documentable, and profitable. If you can find a way to bring your prospects (or prospectors) what they need, consistently and efficiently at a profit, you have a great chance to succeed.

The other thing you need is competitive advantage, but we will go over that later in the book.

Let's talk about positioning. Some of you may have spent a lot of time thinking about this when you started your business. A lot of businesses seem to get this right because that's how their business has survived by slowly working their way into a good position in the marketplace.

The most basic form of product positioning is price versus quality.

Let's make a simple graph. Draw a bottom horizontal line and a vertical line upward from the left edge.

On the left axis put prices for the competing product in your market and on the bottom axis put a quality score from 1 to 10. Then draw a line diagonally across the graph, splitting it into two equal triangles from bottom left to top right.

Your graph should show that the higher the price, the higher the quality should be. (roughly)

Where are you on the quality versus price graph? You should be close to the diagonal line that split the graph into two equally sized triangles.

What if you're not close to the line?

That means you have an issue.

If you are higher quality than most of your competitors and cost less than most of them, then you aren't charging enough.

This is a failure of most freelancers who are trying to get more clients by being better and cheaper than everyone else. But what happens is you don't have a good market fit.

People who want higher quality, don't believe they will get it because your service is too inexpensive.

People who want to pay less but you have promised more, will take advantage of you. You will spend more and more of your time for less money and eventually you will go broke.

You should graph the price and quality of all your competitors and see where the holes in the marketplace are. If there is a big gap in both quality and price somewhere along the middle or top right of the graph, that's the place you want to be.
Price and quality should match.

For other types of marketing positioning, you want to make a product positioning statement.

"For businesses that want to grow and save time, Hook Digital Marketing offers done-for-you marketing and advertising solutions that solve this problem by giving them measurable success at scale without the time and staff overhead of an in-house marketing team."

Now let's make your product positioning statement.

"For *[potential customers]* that *[want/need] [problem/solution]*, *[my company]* offers *[product]* that solves this problem by *[how you solve it]*."

Here's another example:

"For *Pet Businesses* that *have a hard time differentiating themselves from other providers*, *Bark Cartons* offers *paper treat boxes customized with their logo, photo, and contact information* that solves this problem by *giving them a simple give-away with staying power to promote their business*."

And another for a travel agent:

"For *people who want a vacation* that *want a worry free vacation without additional costs*, *All Planned Travel* offers *fully planned trips with air travel, hotel, and other amenities* that solves this problem by *touring the resorts we send our guests, having a direct line to work with airlines, and the experience to be your advocate if you have a problem while away from home*."

This is for your internal use only. This is a statement to guide how you formulate and price your products and services.

This statement can help you decide who your customer avatar is, and what you offer.

It should explain your competitive advantage.

* * *

Timing is hard.

When you are launching a new product or service or running a marketing campaign, you have to get the timing right.

It's important to note that when launching something completely new, you may not be able to test the timing without soft launching your product. *Soft launch* being the term for letting just a few people try it and see how that goes before you spend the time and money to roll it out to everyone.

I *soft launched* this book.

A couple of months ago, I posted the beginning of Chapter 1 on my personal Facebook account. I had some friends read it and comment, "OMG! Am I Janet! Are you writing about me?"

I was able to strike a chord with people, so I knew I should move forward and get the book done. I set an aggressive deadline and here we are.

Later in the book, I'm going to tell you how I was able to use the strategies outlined in this book to write and launch it in 90 days. And it's not a book about *how to write a book*.

Timing matters in the marketplace. If your product or service is too new, you must attempt to convince people to try it out.

If it's too old, there is already an incumbent. Someone else already won the battle and you'll have to woo their customers away from them. Or worse, the service is not something people are buying anymore. Try to open a new cable TV service or cab company and see how that flies.

The second-best timing is to be launching something that is trending but just starting to get popular or necessary.

A good source of trending information is Google Trends. See what people are searching for online.

At the time of writing, CBD oil is trending, as well as eScooters, electric cars, meal box services, grocery delivery, and local SEO, among other things.

The best-timing is to buy the real estate before the destination is popular, to paraphrase Gary Vaynerchuck; To have your product ready to launch just before it's trending so you are ready to capitalize on the demand.

There are also some products that can be launched at any time and the right time for those is now. For example, if you are offering a service to an underserved community or you have found a gap in the market that doesn't have something at the price and quality you can provide it. If you have one of these products, launch now.

And remember that you have to finish something to get it out the door. You have to "ship it."

Seth Godin says "Merely ship it." Meaning that your job isn't to just do amazing work, it's to make work that is the best that can be made at the time you are making it with the resources you have available.

Perfect is the enemy of "done."

If you keep tweaking until something is "perfect" then you will never finish it and you will never bring it to the world. And timing doesn't make any difference if you never launch.

CHAPTER 8
Dealing with Clutter

"Instead of creating an ad campaign that somehow cuts and invades, consider creating a product, a service and a story that we'd miss if we couldn't find it."
—Seth Godin

MOST OF US HAVE BECOME DIGITAL HOARDERS. The digital clutter in our lives and in our cloud-warehoused data is immeasurable by standards used when I was a kid.

People talk about organizing their messy desk, or hiring professional organizers come and turn their spaces into more productive environments. But who is organizing the digital workspace of your business?

When was the last time you looked for something on your computer and didn't know if it was on your computer, another computer in the office, Dropbox, OneDrive, Google Drive, etc.

If those files were actual paper files with important company information or customer data, you would have them well organized and in a locked cabinet or room.

When files are digital and not something you can hold in your hand, they seem less real and we often take less care of these files.

But just ask a company that had a major customer data leak how it turned out for them financially and how people perceive their brand now, and you'll start to wonder if maybe it's time to take better care of your digital paperwork.

Technical jargon alert!

But only enough to know how to speak intelligently about things you need.

* * *

It takes time to clean up your files, but a little organization goes a long way.

For starters. Let's make sure you understand why you need your files organized.

Three reasons.

1. Backups
2. Efficiency
3. Hacking

Most companies I see have several file hoarding issues that are all susceptible to these three problems.

The big one is multiple file storage solutions without any rhyme or reason. Usually created on the fly at one point and then used on and off until they needed more file space and then those become subscription services and now you're paying multiple parties to still not have all your stuff in one place.

Photos on a Dropbox, Office files in OneDrive, some docs and PDFs in a Google Drive, and some stuff in MS Office file shares on the office network.

Which computer are those files on? No one really knows. Your IT guy doesn't even know where all your stuff is. That's a problem. A big problem.

Here's a quick scenario that happened to a client of one of our networking friends.

One of the employees got an email that looked like it came from the owner of the company. They opened the file attachment and it was what looked like a messed up PDF document.

They picked up the phone and called the boss.

"But I never sent you anything…" the boss replies.

By then the virus had time to encrypt all the files on that computer, OneDrive, Dropbox, Google Drive, etc.

All of them.

They would have been completely screwed.

But in this case, the company had a "backup appliance" which is a system that keeps a copy of all their files every day.

They still lost more than a day's worth of work for every person in the office. And they had to pay the IT company to come save the day.

Once a file is encrypted you can't open it or get the contents out until you get what is called an encryption key.

Encryption is what is used to keep documents out of the wrong hands, but often, it's used to ruin people's day and blackmail companies for literally tens of thousands of dollars, if not millions in some cases, to get access to their own files.

Usually once all the files are encrypted and inaccessible, the culprit will blackmail the company for the encryption key. "Pay us $20,000 USD in bitcoin in 48 hours to get access to your files or they will be lost forever."

You don't want to be reading that message.

Now that we have covered hacking...

"But what about backups and efficiency? I thought you just said the backups saved the day."

First off, most of you reading this have no backups. Part of the reason you don't have backups is because you don't know where all your files are. How do you even begin to make backups if you don't know where all your stuff is?

If your company can afford it, or if losing all your digital files would be a doomsday scenario for your business, I recommend talking to an IT company. Get someone who answers the phone quickly. Get references.

This is important, and you don't want to go with the cheapest, you want to go with the most competent.

If you can't get an IT company or if your company doesn't have an internal IT person, then the next best thing you can do is to get all your stuff in one place.

Check the computers of everyone in your computer and make sure no one is hoarding files on their computer where the only existing copy of it resides on their computer. This is a recipe for disaster.

Second, make sure that you choose one cloud-based backup solution that meets your needs and make sure that your subscription level includes backups and quick restore times. Backups are no good if you must wait weeks to get the files back. Also make sure they have encryption protection.

The next thing you need to do is to make sure that all your other previously used file systems are cleaned up. Make sure all the old files and customer data are cleaned out of those places and those accounts are deleted. If you have old customer data on a cloud server you haven't used for a few years and someone breaks into it, you're still liable.

If you are really worried about it, get insurance. You can get insurance to cover data loss and breaches.

Once you have all the files in one place, and the previous used locations all cleaned up, you need to educate your staff. Make sure everyone knows where you are storing stuff and not to store files elsewhere.

Make sure you have antivirus and firewalls between you and the outside world. It's a scary Internet and there's a million nasty things out there just waiting to get into your company and wreak havoc on your already busy schedule.

You think you're busy now, just wait until you need to clean up an infected office full of old PCs.

Finally, efficiency.

Make sure your new file system is well organized. Think of it like departments – each department gets their own folder. Then you can drill down from there.

Just make sure it's organized well and if you have employees make sure they only have access to the folder they need access to.

The "default" for good security is don't give anyone access to anything unless they must have it to do their job. Because someone needs one file, don't give them access to the entire company.

You don't need your intern poking around in your banking and HR files, do you?

Lastly, efficiency.

It's just faster when everyone knows all the files are in one place and they don't have to search around for them.

When I call a client and ask if they have some photos to use for their website or advertising, sometimes it takes them days to find them. That's not efficient.

If anyone asks me for anything, I know where it is. So does my staff. And if we can't find it, there's only one place to search for it. You can then use the built in search function for that platform and find your important digital things in seconds.

* * *

Now let's talk about that old website.

My company makes and re-designs websites all the time and I know what people do with their old website content when they make a new one.

"Copy all the old pages and blogs to the new site and just skin them to the new look!"

As I've said earlier in this book, the Internet is full of spam and garbage. Don't add to it.

Audit your own website content in two easy steps.

Out-dated pages on your website can hurt you. People can get the wrong impression if they find those pages, and it can hurt your search rankings online if old crappy pages are being ranked better than your newer pages.

Step 1 – Browse every page on your website. Every article, every FAQ, every product. If you can't do it all because you have 10,000 products, spot check them.

Step 2 – If it's out of date, update it. If it's no longer needed, delete it. * Make sure you have a backup before you delete anything.

* There are tools you can use to see page views on your website as well as ways to detect which pages appear in search. These pages should either be updated, or you should use what is called a 301 Redirect. It's an SEO thing – if you

don't know what it is, reach out to me and I'll let you know what to do.

Make sure you have a backup of your website. If you have a hosting provider or web-person you use, make sure that they provide you a backup you can keep that isn't on the same server system that the website is on.

This is called an off-site backup. You need one.

Make sure your website software is kept up to date. Especially with websites on WordPress or other builders, someone needs to keep it up to date for security patches. If that's not you, pay someone to do it.

A couple years back a children's psychiatric clinic contacted us because there were links to porn on their website. This happened because it wasn't kept up to date on security patches.

Also, they didn't have a backup.

They didn't know they didn't have a backup. They assumed it came with their expensive hosting. When we called their expensive hosting, the web host staff didn't know there wasn't a backup either.

Don't just trust that it's taken care of, find out.

You're liable, not them.

"Hoping" your website is protected isn't going to give you much solace when potential clients are looking at Viagra links or indecent acts on your business website.

I would also shy away from anywhere that is just a one-man show for hosting your website.

We've had more than a dozen companies unable to get their domain names renewed, get access to their websites, etc. because the person who ran the company hosting it for them literally died. Then when their credit cards stop paying the hosting bill, all their customer's websites go down and no one can get into them.

That's a nightmare you don't want to be calling me about.

Trust me.

Have a backup and make sure security patches are being applied to your website on a regular basis. It's worth it.

CHAPTER 9
Competitive Advantage

"If you don't have a competitive advantage, don't compete."
—Jack Welch

IF YOU DON'T HAVE A CLEAR WAY FOR YOUR CUSTOMERS TO TELL YOU APART FROM YOUR COMPETITION, then you are at the mercy of the marketplace. You don't have a competitive advantage.

What you have is another recipe for disaster.

Let me tell you a story about glow in the dark stars. The kind that go on the ceiling of children's bedrooms. But first, let me ask you a question.

Is there anything stopping a competitor from opening "across the street" from you and taking half your business?

When I say *across the street*, I mean could someone try to woo the same customers you are trying to attract by making themselves seem like a comparable choice to the products or service you offer.

It could be online, or in the same niche or marketplace. Maybe you are the only shop in town for what you do, but could a competitor move here from another place?

It literally happens all the time.

And what we're really talking about here is differentiation. How are you different or better?

And let me point this out now because it can sting a bit, and it's better to just rip the Band-Aid off.

If someone doesn't know who you are or doesn't know your brand, and they see you and your closest competitor, can they tell the difference?

If the logos and company names were switched, would they know the difference?

Are you one of several lawn mowing companies or are you the shining star in a league all your own?

What makes you different in the eyes of your customer?

That my friend, is competitive advantage.

Now, let's talk glow in the dark stars.

I saw a presentation a couple years back about how to do Amazon Drop-Shipping Arbitrage.

That's a mouthful, but what they were talking about is finding something you can buy cheap from Asia and sell it for a profit on Amazon and keep the difference, without buying the product up front.

This guy's top selling product was a box of glow in the dark stars that you can put on your child's bedroom ceiling or in a classroom. There were hundreds of people selling glow in the dark stars.

At the time, the cheapest was 150 glow in the dark stars for $11.99. He made a box with 200 glow in the dark stars, plus a free moon! And it was $11.95.

It was a little more value, for slightly less money. Better product photos, he captured more reviews, had a better product description, etc. And that strategy made him over $1 Million in sales the first year.

Since then a bit of a ceiling-star price war has gone on, but he's still selling them and some variations and doing fine.

The point is the person selling 150 stars for $11.99 didn't know what hit them. Suddenly their million dollar a year money-maker was second fiddle to a new sheriff in town. The *free moon*.

What they had was a cheap way to make glow in the dark stars, what they didn't have was a sustainable competitive advantage.

And someone came along with a better offer and are still eating their lunch to this day.

Competitive advantage can be about price or value, but it's of little consequence if you can't sell that value to the customer.

You can't be a choice in the marketplace, you have to be the best choice for your perfect customer.

Let me tell you a little about my competitive advantage when I talk to my potential customers. The first thing I do when I meet with them is give them a copy of my latest book.

At that point, it's already over for most of my competitors.

I am now the expert in the field, because I wrote a book about it.

Everyone else has an expensive business card, but I wrote the book. The evidence is right there on the table and people who write books are experts in the eyes of people who haven't read the book yet.

Hopefully you will think I am an expert after you read the book too, but we're talking about differentiation right now.

Let's talk for a moment about your website. Does it clearly state what you do and the problem you solve for your customer?

If not, don't worry too much, because your competitor's website probably doesn't either. You'll be in on the coin-flip when potential customers try to choose to use you or them.

Everyone talks about how their fantastic customer service and their experience is their competitive advantage. And it might be, but not until *after* they use your company's service.

When everyone's website and marketing says the same thing, it's not an advantage. It's a lottery.

According to their websites, every realtor treats their clients like family and will negotiate on your behalf to help you with a smooth transaction.

Every plumber, contractor, electrician, roofer, flooring person, masonry builder and handyman has over 10 or 20 years of experience, great service, and is licensed and bonded.

Every carpet cleaner or car detailer or auto mechanic is affordable, professional, and has competitive rates.

When your customer looks on the internet, usually by saying something like "*OK Google/Hey Siri* – carpet cleaners in Hillsboro, Oregon," a list comes up.

And all the listings look the same.

So, what do you do?

You call the first one. You may not even visit their website at all if your device found them for you or the search engine provided the phone number.

If they don't answer and you get their voicemail, you don't leave a message. You call the next one.

And if none of them answer, you might go back and call again and leave a message but more likely, you'll just ask on social media if anyone knows a good carpet cleaner.

With some industry exceptions, you almost never fill out a form on a website anymore. No one really does these days. It's the *phone tree* of the Internet. No one wants to use long contact forms anymore.

You want someone to get the dog-stains out of your rug before your Mother-in-Law comes to town, not fill out a half page form about your residential demographics.

Saying you have great service and experience is the barrier of entry. That just gets you the chance to play in the sandbox. It's not a strategy for winning.

Having those things is still not a winning combination. That's just enough to keep you in the game.

Your product needs to be above average, your price should match, and you are giving your customers something to talk about when you're done. More importantly, you need to be giving them a reason to choose you over a competitor.

And being cheaper is almost always a failure, because someone else can always do it cheaper. And if they can't, they will be able to soon. There's always more innovation or a new process, or even a company willing to come into your market and lose money just to gain market share.

Ask any local store what happened when Walmart came to town. And ask the Waltons what happened when Amazon came to town.

I talked to a guy who was going to sell makeup to young women online. The first thing he did was sell 2 make-up brushes for $4 with free shipping. He lost $2/customer.

Why would he do that?

He did it because the incumbent in the marketplace selling similar brushes was selling one brush for $4, plus a couple bucks for shipping. His product was wining the price war, and the other guys couldn't compete.

Fact is, he didn't care about the brushes at all. He was spending $2 to get the email address of a woman who was likely to purchase his makeup products soon. He makes the money on the makeup; the brushes are just a lost leader.

He wasn't selling brushes at all; he was buying market share of *people likely to purchase makeup.* In the process, he put the other cheap makeup brush folks out of business. In a race to the bottom, the only thing worse than winning is going broke coming in second place.

Take the high ground. Don't compete on price.

Studies have shown that 20-30% of people in any market shop on price alone and no other features, benefits, or other advantages will change their mind. So don't deal with them.

Do you know what our salespeople say when a potential customer low-balls them on a price and says they can get that price elsewhere?

"That's a great deal, you should take it."

Our price includes us. And no one else has our people and talent. If someone wants a bargain, go get one. There's a million people out there willing to work cheaper. Come back and tell me how it worked out.

Usually these types of customers just aren't a good fit for our business anyway, and probably aren't for yours either.

Businesses that pay for quality expect a certain level of knowledge, experience, and expertise. They know it isn't cheap.

If they want that expertise without paying for it, then they don't understand pricing and they aren't going to be in business too long anyway.

Unless you have something no one else can get, such as very specific talent, protected secrets or trademarks, political or legal protections, or access to capital so that you can lose money to gain market share, then you need a new strategy to win.

Differentiation is that strategy.

Fitting in as a brand or a freelancer in the crowded marketplace we live in now is marketing suicide.

If someone searches and gets a list of results that all look the same, they just pick the first one.

If someone looks for a product you sell on a marketplace like Amazon, and yours doesn't speak to a specific need, then they just sort by price. Because if they are all the same, why look further?

Maybe you already have a well-defined competitive advantage. But do your customers agree with you? Have you surveyed them? How did they find you and why did they choose you?

The next question is this. Is your advantage a sustainable competitive advantage? How long will it last?

For every Uber, there is a Lyft waiting in the wings.

Once someone makes something that works, it's easier to replicate it.

One thing that's hard to replicate is reputation. Another is differentiation, as long as that difference is hard to replicate.

A hard to replicate differentiator is you. Especially if you are a freelancer.

You are different than other people. Use your quirks and personality to differentiate you. Most people hide that they are a one-person show and hide behind websites and language to make them look like a larger company.

Don't do that. Be you.

If you have a larger company though, you need to watch out for the *dancing bear syndrome*. You don't want to be the star of the show, trapped and unable to leave because when you stop "dancing" the money stops coming in.

I can't tell you what your competitive advantage is. You need to find that for yourself. If you don't have one, you need to make one.

It could be your personal network, an upgrade to your offering, strategic partnerships, or a myriad of other things. Seek it out, then test it with your prospects and customers and see if it helps them purchase from you or stay with you longer.

* * *

Let's talk about something no one wants to talk about.

Why customers leave.

No one likes to feel like a failure and often that is what we feel like when customers leave us. Or we blame them.

The fact is most customers leave for the same three reasons.

First though, a couple points on why unhappy customers don't leave.

- The cost of switching is too high or difficult.
- You are the only game in town.

In either of these cases, as soon as a competitor shows up, you're out.

This means that the cost of switching is a competitive advantage but only if someone else isn't showing up to compete with you and help your customer leave.

Now back to why customers leave.

Most studies agree that about 10% of customers left because they were persuaded to use a competitor.

About 14% leave because they are unhappy with the product or service.

And 68% leave because they believe the brand or service provider doesn't care about them.

Sixty-eight percent.

Do you know what this means?

Caring about your customers is important but *showing them you care* is a competitive advantage.

When I worked selling electronics in the 90s, we had a promotion at the store that every new customer received a cool little clock radio. It was the 90s and clock radios were still popular.

One of my best customers came up to me during the promotion and asked if he could have a clock radio. He did spend thousands of dollars at the store, with me, and that matters even more when we work on commissions.

I gave him one.

I wasn't supposed to.

My manager officially reprimanded me and was angry to the point of yelling because I gave one of my best repeat customers a promotional item that was only to be given to new customers.

What do you think would have happened if I didn't give him one?

What if I didn't give him one and he went to a competing store a few blocks away, and they gave him one?

We need to make sure we aren't only speaking to our customers when we are trying to woo them into giving us their money.

How many companies do you pay right now for services that only send you an email or call you if your payment was late, your card expired, or they want to sell you more things?

Building a relationship without your hand in your customer's wallet is a modern competitive advantage.

In a world of automated upsells, robo-calls, and email blasts, maybe it's time to talk to your customers more and let them know you still care.

CHAPTER 10
All Advice is Not Created Equal

"Most great people have attained their greatest success just one step beyond their greatest failure."
—Napoleon Hill

IF YOU MAKE A NEW WEBSITE OR FLYER FOR YOUR BUSINESS AND SHOW IT TO TEN NON-BUSINESS OWNERS, most of them will tell you something is wrong with it. The real problem is, they don't know what they're talking about.

I don't say that in a mean way. They just aren't designers or marketing professionals. Sure, everyone has seen a logo or a website, we see them all the time. But that's doesn't make everyone an expert on branding, design, and copywriting. I drive a car every day and it doesn't make me a mechanic.

When you make something new - a logo, a flyer, a website, a product or service, make sure the people whose opinion you are getting are the ones who are either experts in that thing, or people who are going to be paying you to use the product.

Your Aunt Lilly may be great at telling you that she liked your blue background website better, or that maybe the boutique service you have developed is something, "no one would pay for."

She's probably wrong.

Often when you are asking people to give you their opinion, you are probably looking for confirmation, but they are hearing, "Tell me what you think is wrong with this."

Your friends and family usually aren't your target market either. I can count on one hand the number of people I know who understand how to make a Facebook ad. If they aren't in the target market of the advertisement I am making, their opinion probably isn't going to make it better.

They want to help, but their opinion is only valuable in the fact that it makes them feel like they are helping you and possibly saving you money or mistakes.

If they aren't business owners or entrepreneurs, they aren't going to be looking at the world through the same lens you do.

I recently was going to the park with my wife and my daughter and she pointed out the other parents there, mentioning, "We might have to make small talk with them."

I told her that sometimes I don't think I'm "good at having a conversation with consumers."

I accidentally called my neighbors "consumers."

Maybe I am working too much, but maybe I understand that we're just not all playing in the same sandbox.

Business owners, entrepreneurs, executives, and committed team members are a special breed.

They are the ones who don't punch the clock to get out of work as quickly as possible. We're building something, not just *putting in our time.*

Maybe you have a *side hustle*. Maybe you are working toward opening a business and you need to punch a clock for a while. There's absolutely nothing wrong with that.

Maybe you are part of a growing business and are an integral part of a great team. You don't need to be a boss to be part of building something awesome.

And that's the goal, right?

Not just putting in your time to get wages. You want to build something bigger than yourself. You want to be able to grow your business, to scale it, or even getting to the point that your business runs itself without you.

Don't worry if Aunt Lily or Carol from the daycare don't think your new service is something anyone would pay for.

It's not for them. They aren't your target customer.

They aren't going to buy a car that costs more than their house, but people who can afford them buy cars that expensive every day.

Maybe your sister in law likes the icon in cornflower blue and doesn't realize that it's the words on a website that make the sales.

Uncle Mickey will tell you Bitcoin is worthless while he's got a pocket full of lottery tickets.

Alfonzo might tell you everyone will just buy insurance from Geico anyway, so why bother becoming an agent.

Harriet will tell you that spending on AM radio and newspaper ads is the way to find new customers. "No one but Millennial kids use them phones anyhow."

There's a lot more bad advice than good advice. Try to find someone who's been there before in your industry or a related one and have them put a second set of eyes on whatever you need help with.

Business networking group peers are great for advice, so are business coaches who have run businesses as well.

Skip the gurus taking photos in front of their AirBnB rented houses and rented Lambo's. You don't need that kind of B.S. in your life.

If it's a product for customers, pick a few of your customers and give them a sneak peak at the new product or service and see what they think. If you are in development, maybe have a quick coffee or call with a couple of them and explain the idea.

Your customers are a fountain of useful information and the more you listen to them, the better you will be able to fit your products to their needs.

The important thing here is to listen. *Really listen.* But before you do, make sure the voice you're listening to is a voice that matters, and not just someone who likes to hear themselves speak.

When it comes to social media and looking for advice from people you don't know, opinions are like assholes;

everybody's got one and they should keep that shit to themselves.

If you can find someone who's been where you need to get to, do whatever you can to help that person in exchange for some advice.

Because opinions from the right source are a gold mine.

CHAPTER 11
The Critical Path

"Operations keeps the lights on, strategy provides a light at the end of the tunnel, but project management is the train engine that moves the organization forward."
— Joy Gumz

AN ALMOST UNIMAGINABLE AMOUNT OF MONEY AND PRODUCTIVITY IS LOST IN BUSINESSES BECAUSE PEOPLE DON'T KNOW WHAT THEY SHOULD DO NEXT. The act of figuring out what to do is probably costing your business a fortune.

Just like confusion is the enemy of good marketing, confusion is the enemy of productivity for yourself and your staff. You need to attempt to have as much clear direction as you can to help keep your employees and yourself on the *critical path.*

The critical path means the steps it takes to reach a goal or milestone. Let's start with something really simple.

My wife Kari wanted to learn how to run.

She knew how to run, as in, "run away from something," but she wanted to know how to become a runner.

She had read about people who were into running, she knew people who loved running, and she watched a couple documentaries about runners, but she didn't really get it. She hated the thought of running.

The first thing she did was download an app called "Couch to 5k," while sitting on the couch. So she literally was at the first step.

Then she had to get some shoes, check!

Then it was a little walking and a very short run that was short but exhausting. Running a block was a real chore, but she stuck to it.

A few days later, the app has her walking a little less and running a little more. Then half walking and half running. Pretty soon, she's running the whole way.

A couple months later, she signed up for a 5K race and was able to run the whole thing.

From there she trained more and got some more running gear she needed to go further. It was four miles, then six and then eight and so on. Pretty soon she ran a half marathon.

Less than a year from her first couch to 5k, she ran a full marathon.

But how is that possible? She was sitting on the couch and hating running less than 12 months ago?

She had discovered the critical path.

Each step needed to get to the finish line of the marathon was dependent on the previous step.

She just got back yesterday (as I am writing this chapter) from doing the *Portland to Coast*. A relay race from Portland, Oregon, to the Pacific Coast with a team of 12 people. After each section of running/walking the person hands off the baton to the next person until the baton passes 131 miles, all the way to the beach in Seaside, Oregon.

It takes planning, preparation, teamwork and each step depends on the last. The result is a feat no single runner in their group could have accomplished.

This is the idea of the critical path. How to create something one step at a time and know what is going to happen next. It's a relay race. You can't finish the next step until you do the previous one.

The critical path in your company needs four things.

1. A Goal.
2. A team that knows what to do next.
3. Someone who figures out what the steps are.

4. A champion for the project to manage it, monitor it, and get it across the finish line.

For example, let's say your goal was to create a newsletter for your customers as our example.

First off, you need to understand the goal and define it.

"We want to send a newsletter to all our existing customers, every week, to help keep them as customers longer and make sure all the departments have input on it."

You take the goal and you work backwards until you get to the starting point, which is where you are now. Make sure you document all the steps.

- Before the newsletter goes out, we need to know what it is going to say. Someone needs to write the content.
- We need to write the newsletter each week, so we need to set aside time on the calendar to write it.
- We need to know what we are going to talk about in the newsletter, so we will need to have a meeting to collect everyone's ideas. Once a

month we can get the stakeholders together and nail this down.
- If we are going to send emails out, we need a way to send them. We will need to research and signup with an email provider.
- We need to make sure that we can export the names and emails of our customers out of our sales system and get them into a list.
- Someone needs to oversee getting everyone together and making final decisions. We need to find this person and brief them on the next steps.
- We need to approve any funding or expenditures or costs related to writing the newsletters, graphic design, etc.
- Have a meeting with sales and marketing to discuss the decision to move forward on the project.

Once you have a plan, you can start from the beginning, and work your way up the list. You can identify what has dependencies and what can be done in parallel, assign the resources needed, etc.

Create a plan. Work the plan.

This works for anything in any industry.

If you were building a house, you don't build the roof before you order the shingles. You have things that need to be done in order, and on time. Each delay in a dependent task pushes back the timeline on everything that follows it.

If the lumber for your walls didn't show up on time, it doesn't matter if the roofing people show up, you don't have any walls to build the roof on yet.

You want to try to account for any potential delays in the plan. This is sometimes called "padding" your time, or "leaving slack in the system."

You want to plan for delays early, because you can't make up the time when it's too late.

* * *

Earlier, I mentioned that my toddler, Faith, loves the show Boss Baby: Back in Business. The vague goal of Baby Corp ™ is to increase the amount that people in the world love babies, so that people love babies more than anything else.

The Boss Baby tells his intern, "Superfat Mailroom Intern Baby" (yes, that's his name) that every time he does a task, he should ask himself one question.

"How does this increase baby love?"

This is about aligning with your company's mission. Anything that helps the company accomplish that mission is what I would call being on the critical path, though in this case, it's really more of a specific path, in a project management sense of the phrase.

Maybe *on-mission* would be a better phrase for this, but however you label it, everyone in your business should understand what your brand stands for and what you are trying to accomplish.

Anyone who is not on the critical path, needs to either get out of the way, or assist those that are on the critical path.

If someone is working on something to move the mission of the company forward or doing an important and dependent step in the path to an important goal, you need to make sure their distractions are limited, and they get whatever help they need to succeed.

Software, entertainment, event management, catering, just to name a few, are businesses where timing is crucial and being late means failure, and in some cases could mean bankruptcy. In these cases, ensuring everyone on the critical path gets all the help they need and the quiet and focus they need is vital.

Find any way you can to limit distractions and increase support to those on the critical path for your business.

And always ask yourself, *"How does this increase baby love?"*

CHAPTER 12
The Final Countdown: Deadlines Get Things Done

"Dreams without deadlines are dead in the water. Deadlines are really lifelines to achieving our goals."
—Irving Wallace

PARKINSON'S LAW IS THE ADAGE THAT WORK WILL EXPAND TO FILL THE AVAILABLE TIME FOR ITS COMPLETION. In other words, if you set long deadlines, the tasks will take that long.

I set aggressive deadlines. I don't set unrealistic deadlines, though some people may think they are unrealistic. They are realistic to me because I understand the critical path and I can see what time is available in my schedule because of time blocking.

Almost everyone I've ever met who is a business professional has been told they need to block their time. Basically, this just means scheduling time for tasks and not just scheduling appointments.

Not just meetings and appointments. Schedule time to do work. If you answer emails for the first two hours of your workdays (which I wouldn't suggest) then block that time out as "email answering" on your calendar.

If you generally return phone calls in the afternoon, you schedule "phone call" time. It's all straightforward.

It saves you time because you know what you must do and when to do it. Remember earlier when we were talking about how much time is wasted by people trying to figure out what they should be doing?

If you schedule too much or too little time for certain tasks, just adjust as needed.

The next thing you need to do is to schedule time to get things done that will move your business forward.

Putting them on your schedule is like putting a big rock in a stream. The water/work will just flow around it.

Schedule a time in your calendar for marketing/sales tasks or time to invent or innovate, depending on what you do and what moves your company forward.

You also need to schedule at least 1-2 hours every week for time to spend on what some call "special projects." These are tasks you know would help your business grow, but you just never get around to.

I'm talking about tasks that need a specifically scheduled distraction-free time to work on them. Blocking this time on my calendar is how we got our blog and Medium publications going. It's how we started our podcast. It's how we started our own networking group. If we didn't schedule time to work on these special projects, they would never have gotten off the ground.

You have blocked time for tasks, and calls, and email, and special projects, and your normal meetings and appointments, now what?

Now you know how much time is left over. It probably isn't a lot. And you probably need to keep some open time available for meetings or to put out fires. You should always build some slack into the system.

This left-over time is the amount you have remaining to set a deadline and accomplish something. Maybe that something is what you came up with during your special projects time or it's something you've been meaning to do for ages and just never got around to.

If you have an extra couple of hours a week and you have a project that will take 10 hours to complete, you will need to schedule 2 hours a week for 5 weeks to finish that project. If you want to "pad" your deadline a bit in case of unexpected delays, set the deadline 6 weeks out.

Voila. You now have a deadline to get something done that you've been meaning to do for ages.

And you have to respect the calendar.

You must let everyone else know that they need to respect your calendar also.

If someone is habitually late, stop waiting for them. Just leave. Tell them they have to reschedule. They will stop being late to your appointments. If someone schedules over your blocked time without a valid reason, you must tell them they need to reschedule it.

Time blocking is about respecting your time. It's about getting the important work done. Work that's on the critical path forward.

And the reason you have to stay late at the office every day, or that you can't take a vacation is that you aren't prioritizing your time and blocking it out in your calendar and then refusing to let those appointments be pushed around.

There is no such thing as, "I don't have time for that."

What you're actually saying is, "I have something more important to do."

A lot of time what you are currently doing seems more urgent but if you were to calculate the opportunity cost, you would see that maybe the most urgent thing isn't the most important.

If a *perfect customer* called up and wanted to meet with you for lunch to close a big deal, but you generally don't go to lunch out of the office, would you do it?

Yes. Because that's a big deal.

But if it was for something trivial, you wouldn't, because, "you don't have time for that."

The fact is, you do have time for that. You're just rightfully choosing to do something else. You are weighing the opportunity costs and choosing to work on something that is on the critical path to move your business forward; something is of greater long-term value.

If you don't set deadlines, things don't get done because there is never any real motivation to get it finished. There is no urgency.

Also, as a business leader, you must set the example. If you don't respect your deadlines, your employees won't either.

Everyone involved needs to be accountable for the entire team's deadlines. If someone misses a deadline, you should have distracted them less or helped them more.

You may not always hit a deadline, but you have to try your hardest. And when you don't hit it, you will need to debrief your team (or analyze what happened yourself) and see what went wrong so you can plan accordingly next time.

* * *

You need to make it a matter of culture in your company that you are a group of people who respect time and deadlines, and you get things done.

You can save time on sales and marketing because you understand who your customer is and where you can reach out to them. You can build relationships and do work that compounds over time instead of constantly trying to figure out what you're supposed to be doing next.

Use simple tools like ICCE and ARMAR to know what you need to work on, and time block these special projects to grow your business.

You will keep yourself and your team on the critical path. Every member of your team will understand that if they aren't on that path right now, they will help those that are when they can and otherwise, stay out of their way.

You will get better results for your clients because you know them better. You can give them better results because you have a more predictable schedule. And you can then create processes and procedures to keep them happy and show them you care because you understand opportunity costs and that it costs 5x as much to get a new customer as it does to keep one you already have.

That time-blocked schedule allows you to work *on your business* every week instead of always just working in it.

Time blocking gives you back the time you need to be creative and find new ways to serve your customers, new streams of revenue, and better ways to attract your perfect clients.

It's time you got your business growing again while working less hours.

Because you and Janet both need a vacation.

Now go forth and be profitable.

CHAPTER 13
The Chapter I Wrote After the Book Was "Done"

> *"nobody can save you but yourself and you're worth saving. It's a war not easily won but if anything is worth winning then this is it."*
> —Charles Bukowski

ONE OF THE HARDEST THINGS TO WRAP OUR BRAINS AROUND IS THE FACT THAT WE ALL FEEL WE NEED SOMEONE ELSE TO CHOOSE US, SOMEONE TO SAVE US. And we don't.

No one is going to save you but yourself.

I don't mean that in a depressing or sad way, but in a way that is empowering.

You are empowered when you are no longer a victim of circumstance, but a survivor who battles adversity and meets challenges, staring them in the face and saying, "I will overcome."

Doing something new or building something better means taking a stand and saying, "I refuse to be mediocre."

It takes guts to stand out.

It takes the guts to say to the world, "I have made this thing and I want you to be a part of it."

It takes courage to be the best leader you can be. It takes courage to create a business that changes culture or serves a need in a way that changes people's lives.

Creating art requires courage.

Think of your business as an art and you are the artist.

Not everyone likes the same art. Remember that regardless of what you make, if someone doesn't hate it, you're probably not making art. If something you make is good for everyone, it's probably not perfect for anyone either.

Creating something great requires courage to ignore the haters and the ones whose advice isn't coming from a place of experience or knowledge.

Building something great needs buy-in from your perspective customers. And that's a lot easier to get if you understand that you are solely responsible for the success of your business.

The only person you need to choose you is your customers.

Imposter syndrome is a real thing and you need to fight it. From time to time most people think they "aren't worthy" or asks themselves, "What makes me so special that I can do ____?"

I listened to a presentation at a business event by someone who built a billion-dollar company. He mentioned that sometimes he doesn't think he has the knowledge and experience to be giving advice to business leaders.

The host of the Business Lunch podcast, Roland Frasier, has built and had profitable exits on more than a dozen multi-million-dollar companies. He still talks about his own Imposter Syndrome. No matter how much success you have, it's always going to be there creeping around in the shadows. Don't ever let it stop you.

You don't need someone to choose you.

Almost all the gatekeepers are gone now.

Just 20 years ago you couldn't publish a book, make a record, get on the radio, be in publication without passing through the gatekeepers who had to pick you.

If they didn't pick you, you didn't get to do that thing.

Thanks to the Internet, anyone can publish a book, start a podcast, have their own "TV" station, or get the word out about what they do, with very few barriers to entry.

Anyone with a credit card can access the most powerful advertising and artificial intelligence systems ever created. Pick up your phone and you have a direct line to 5+ Billion people.

But the problem is that everyone else does too and that makes it really hard to stand out of the vast pool of noise that is growing exponentially.

That's why you need to be an artist.

You need to be an artist and then you need to "find the others," as Seth Godin would say. You need to take what you do and make it perfect for a specific group of people and then put your art into the world.

The "walled gardens" of the Internet are being set up, and that trend will continue. The Wild West days of everyone having access to everyone else is not going to last forever.

New gatekeepers are always building new gates to try to grab power over industries, speech, and access to products and information.

New opportunities from new technologies will keep arriving at an even more frantic pace but if you're an artist, it's very hard to be disrupted. No one "disrupted" Picasso or Mozart.

Be an artist and make your art.

And remember that no one needs to choose you. Now YOU can choose you.

Be your own knight in shining armor, because no one needs to come save you if you're choosing yourself.

MORE HELP TO DO GREAT THINGS

Reading

Start Saying Yes: Improving Customer Experience and Sales Through Positive Messaging

https://amzn.to/3299Owi

Weekly Marketing Tips Right to Your Inbox

https://hookseo.com

Listening

Digital Marketing Masters Podcast
– anywhere you listen to great podcasts!

https://hookseo.com/podcast

www.ingramcontent.com/pod-product-compliance
Lightning Source LLC
Chambersburg PA
CBHW030014190526
45157CB00016B/2696